Let's Talk About Tongues

By Allan Fowler

Consultants

Linda Cornwell, Learning Resource Consultant,
Indiana Department of Education

Fay Robinson, Child Development Specialist

Lynne Kepler, Educational Consultant

Children's Press®
A Division of Grolier Publishing
New York   London   Hong Kong   Sydney
Danbury, Connecticut

Project Editor: Downing Publishing Services
Designer: Herman Adler Design Group
Photo Researcher: Caroline Anderson

Library of Congress Cataloging-in-Publication Data

Fowler, Allan.
    Let's talk about tongues / by Allan Fowler.
      p. cm. – (Rookie read-about science)
    Includes index.
    Summary: Defines the physical characteristics and uses of human and
animal tongues, as well as other meanings of a word that can describe
a language or part of a shoe.
    ISBN 0-516-20324-X (lib.bdg.)   0-516-26157-6 (pbk.)
    1. Tongue—Juvenile literature. [l. Tongue.] I. Title. II. Series
QM503.F68   1997   96-28765
591.4'3–dc20   CIP
                                      AC

Talking about tongues . . .
Did you ever think about
how many ways you use
your tongue?

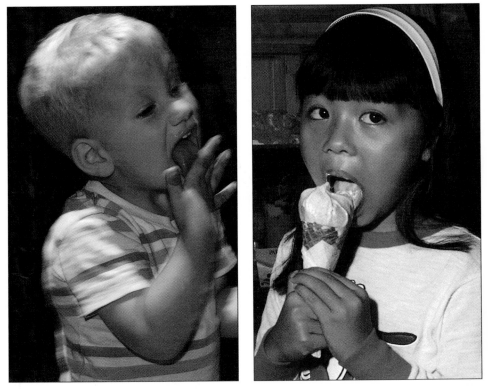

You use it for tasting.
Without your tongue,
food would have no flavor.
Eating would be dull.

Tiny taste buds cover
your tongue.

The buds at the front of
your tongue recognize
only sweet or salty tastes.

The buds on the sides of your tongue are only for sour tastes.

And those at the back
are only for bitter tastes.
The center of your tongue
doesn't taste anything.

With all your taste
buds working together,
you can enjoy the many
delicious flavors of a
chicken dinner . . .

or of an ice cream sundae.

You also use your tongue for talking. You must move it around to form words.

Try reading this sentence out loud while holding your tongue still.

Can't do it, can you?

That's why someone who has trouble speaking is said to be "tongue-tied."

A sentence like "She sells seashells by the seashore" is called a "tongue-twister."

Can you say it ten times — fast — without stumbling?

When a wrong word comes out of your mouth, you say, "It was a slip of the tongue."

People who blow wind
instruments, such as
trumpets, need their
tongues to make sounds.

You need your tongue to
lick stamps and envelopes.
(Well, yes, you *could* use
a sponge.)

Cats wash themselves by licking with their tongues. But people have other ways of keeping clean.

Mammals, birds, and most
fish have tongues.

A giraffe can stick its
tongue out very far to
eat leaves off trees.

chameleon

Certain animals use their
tongues not only to eat
their dinner . . . but to
catch it.

Anteaters and aardvarks
pick up ants, termites,
or grubs with their long,
sticky tongues.

giant anteater

A frog or toad can zap
a fly with its tongue.

iguana

Reptiles also have tongues.

Snakes can even smell with their tongues. A snake's tongue is forked; its end is split in two.

The word "tongue"
has other meanings
besides the pink thing
attached to the bottom
of your mouth.

A language, such as
English or Spanish, is
often called a tongue.

Some kinds of shoes
have tongues.

Can you tell why these
things are called tongues?

There is still another
use for one's tongue.

People have been known
to stick out their tongues
to show they are not
pleased by something
or someone.

But that's considered rude.

So you never do it, do you?

Words You Know

tongue

taste buds

trumpet

anteater

giraffe

reptile

snake

toad

Index

About the Author

Allan Fowler is a free-lance writer with a background in advertising.
Born in New York, he lives in Chicago now and enjoys traveling.

Photo Credits

Photo Researchers, Inc. — ©Stephen Dalton, cover; ©S. Lousada/Petit Format, 6
©Photri, Inc. — 3 (both pictures), 28
Peter Arnold, Inc. — ©Richard Choy, 4; ©S. J. Krasemann, 19, 31 (middle left);
©BIOS (A. Visage)
©Rigoberto Quinteros — 5, 7, 9, 10, 13, 16, 27, 30 (top right)
Valan Photos — ©Kennon Cooke, 11; ©Francis Lepine, 15, 30 (bottom right);
©James R. Page, 17; ©John Fowler, 24, 31 (bottom left); ©V. Wilkinson, 30 (left)
Animals Animals — ©Patti Murray, 18; ©M. Austerman, 21, 31 (top);
©G. I. Bernard/Oxford Scientific Films, 22, 31 (bottom right); ©Sig Leszczynski,
23, 31 (middle right)
Cover: A European toad feeding